HOPE IT ALL WORKS OUT!

A "POORLY DRAWN LINES"
COLLECTION

REZA FARAZMAND

Andrews McMeel
PUBLISHING®

Get It Together

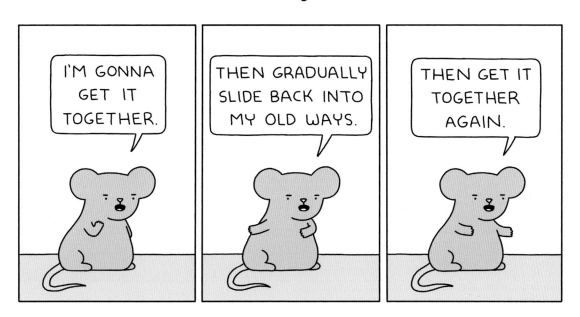

Empty

Work Hard

Come With Me

Think Hard

Trash Bird

Who We Are

Retiring

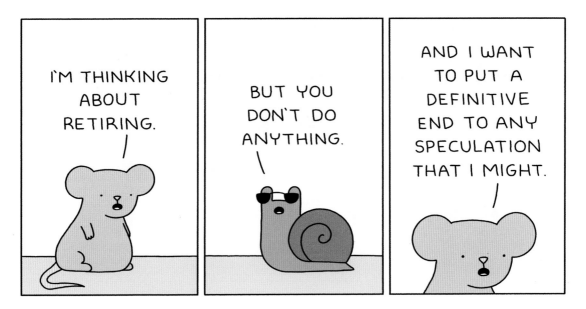

Been Thinking

Ever Feel

The Past

Thank Me Later

Best Friend

Alone

Busy Day

That Hat

Interesting People

Running

Duties As Fish

My Friends

Another Mess

More Decisive

To-Do List

How's Life

All My Clothes

A Trip

We're Off

Self-Doubt

SOMETIMES I HAVE MOMENTS OF SELF-DOUBT.

AM I... <u>TOO</u> INCREDIBLE?

Been Places

Okay

Been a Fish

35

Authenticity

Need to Focus

Found the Ocean

Over This

Future Mouse

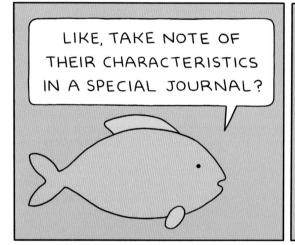

A Mistake

Plan

Ask Too Much

Improve

Sunlight

THE
COLLECTED
SAGA OF
DR. MOUNTAINSON

CHAPTER 1
INTRODUCTIONS

CHAPTER 2
THE TEAM

CHAPTER 3

RETURN
TO THE
MOUNTAIN

PREVIOUSLY...

AND NOW...

THE END?

A Badder Mouse

Been Real

My Best Friends

All the Places

A Break

A Pond

67

Changes

Natural Enemies

How You Want

Do Something

Looking

Knows My Name

One Day

THE MANY FACES OF MOUSE

OVERJOYED

UNDERWHELMED

GOING THROUGH IT

KEEPING IT TOGETHER

CONFUSED

CONFIDENT

SUSPICIOUS

GOING THROUGH IT AGAIN

Just Ask

A Snake

LATER...

Little Bird

Hoops

83

Dog-tor

SO I GUESS YOU'RE A "DOG-TOR" HUH?

I WENT TO MEDICAL SCHOOL, SIR.

Later...

DEAR DIARY,
I MADE A FOOL OF MYSELF TODAY. I WILL TRY TO LEARN AND GROW AS A PERSON FROM THIS.

Nineties Called

Think

Everything Cool

The Smartest

I'M PROBABLY THE SMARTEST ONE HERE.

I THOUGHT YOU WERE THE MOST IGNORANT.

THAT'S WHAT YOU THOUGHT.

BUT YOU DIDN'T THOUGHT ENOUGH.

Made Mistakes

Eat Cheese

Here's Where

Nothing Scares Me

Please Rate

Keeps You Going

Everything

Fly

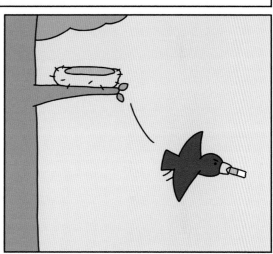

Get Serious

Bird's Request

Get Out of Town

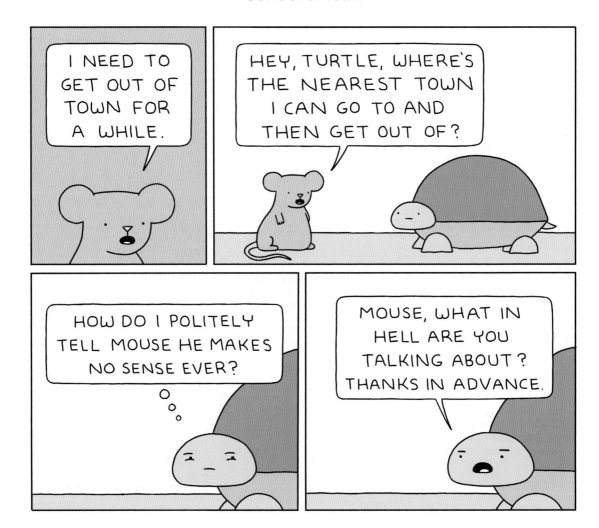

Like Me

Nothing Done

Unusual

A Compliment

Can't Believe

Let Go

Leaving

ALRIGHT, I'M LEAVING.

WHERE ARE YOU GOING?

AND WILL YOU MISS US?

I'LL MISS MOUSE THE MOST. HE'S BEEN MY BRO AND MY BOY, AND I OWE MUCH OF MY HAPPINESS TO HIM.

YESSS.

I'LL MISS SNAIL THE LEAST. I'LL THINK OF HIM FROM TIME TO TIME, THOUGH NOT ALWAYS WITH FONDNESS.

FAIR.

I'LL MISS TURTLE THE MIDDLE MOST. SHE IS CHILL AND DEPENDABLE, AND I KNOW THAT IN TIME WE'D BE THE GREATEST OF PALS.

I KNOW THAT IN TIME AS WELL.

OKAY, SEE YOU ALL IN A COUPLE HOURS.

A COUPLE HOURS LATER...

I'M BACK FROM MY HAIRCUT.

DUDE, NO.

My Shit Together

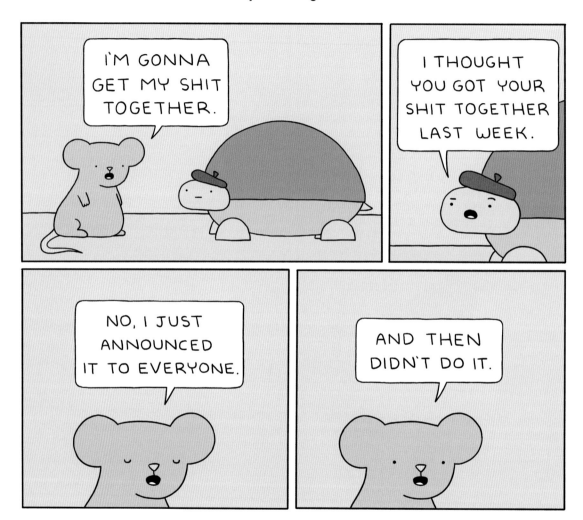

SEAHORSE

Ghosts

Getting Mad

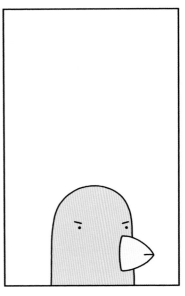

In Thought

The Perfect Bird

Get to Work

Make Friends

Devil's Advocate

RATE YOUR PROBLEMS!
I'M HAVING...

A HARD DAY

A TOUGH WEEK

A DIFFICULT MONTH

A TRYING EXISTENCE

Stronger

Have Your Back

Grudge

So Much

Successful

To the Moon

Sad

The Good Times

An Exchange

Be Mad

Better

What Is It

So Serious

Real

Doing Well

'Til the End

Powerless

Someone

More Relaxed

A New Day

The Robot's Job

Start Trying

The Times

So Tired

This One Goes Out

Some Advice

SNAIL, CAN I GIVE YOU SOME ADVICE?

MOUSE, I'VE HEARD A LOT OF ADVICE.

AND NONE OF IT HAS WORKED ON ME SO FAR.

I'LL TAKE THE ADVICE.

MOUSE, GIVE THE ADVICE TO TURTLE.

QUICKLY! BEFORE BIRD WANTS IT!

UHH—

WAIT NO GIVE IT TO ME!

Mad At You

Habit

A Challenge

Couldn't Help It

Understand Things

Brave

All Your Money

Choose

Everything Is Changing

Work On Myself

I'M GOING TO START WORKING ON MYSELF.

UP UNTIL NOW I'VE BEEN WORKING ON SNAIL.

HOW'D THAT GO?

SNAIL, SHOW HIM.

HE GLOWS WITH RADIANT ENERGY NOW. AND HE CAN LEVITATE.

OKAY, BUT DID HE FIGURE OUT HIS PERSONAL ISSUES?

OH, NO. NO, NO, NO.

NO WAY, MAN.

THOSE RUN DEEP.

A Cat

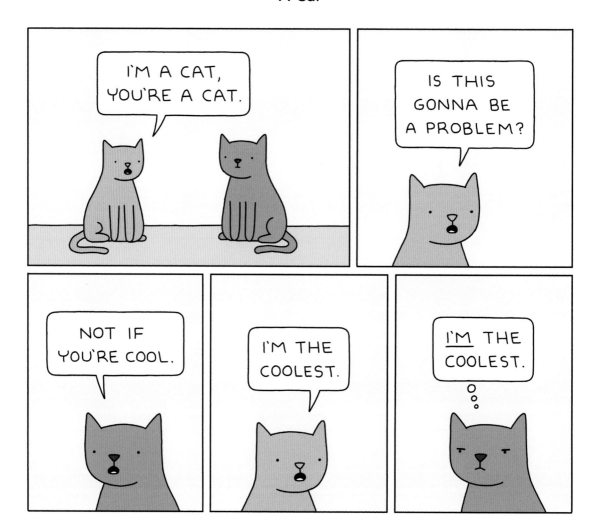

Serpent King

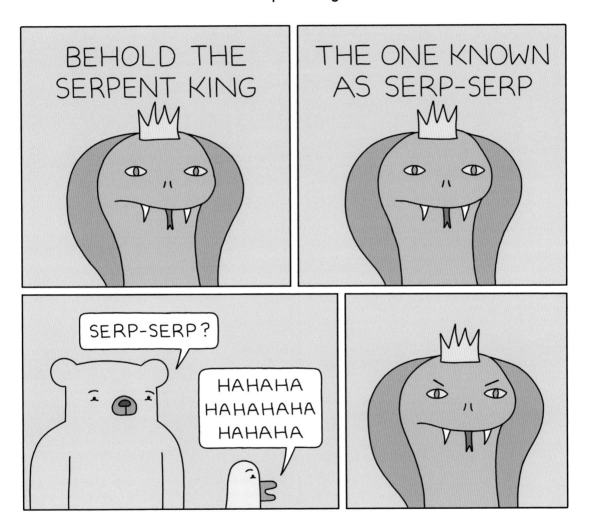

Unstoppable

Saw a Cat

What You're Doing

Whole New Day

Where Is Everyone

You Might

Who I Am

No Free Time

Knife

I CAN'T FIND MY KNIFE.

SNAIL, STOP LEAVING YOUR KNIFE AROUND! IT'S DANGEROUS.

AM I... PART OF THE PROBLEM?

YOU'RE LITERALLY THE ENTIRE PROBLEM.

HEY LOOK, I FOUND A KNIFE.

HUP

I KNEW THIS IS HOW MOUSE WOULD DIE.

MAYBE I AM PART OF THE PROBLEM.

TIME TO SHOOT THIS KNIFE.

OKAY, THAT ONE'S NOT ON ME.

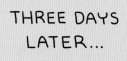
THREE DAYS LATER...

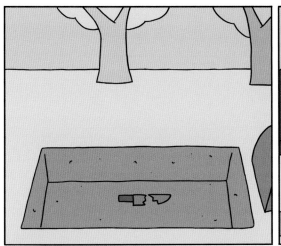

I'M REALLY SORRY I SHOT YOUR KNIFE, SNAIL.

NO, IT'S MY FAULT. THIS WAS A WAKE-UP CALL.

YEAH, SO I GUESS YOU LEARNED YOUR LESSON, SNAIL.

BIRD, COME ON. WE'RE AT HIS KNIFE'S FUNERAL.

SHOW SOME CLASS, BIRD.

IN MEMORIAM SNAIL'S KNIFE

Older

Excuse Me

Unreliable

Your Issues

HOW DO <u>YOU</u>
DEAL WITH
YOUR ISSUES?

Favorite Things

History of Humans

Thinking About

Won't Sit

Turtle Sunset

I WONDER IF THERE ARE OTHER TURTLES WATCHING THIS SUNSET...

ELSEWHERE...

...IN AN AREA THAT ALSO HAS TURTLES BUT THEY'RE LESS POETIC ABOUT THESE THINGS...

WOW, I DON'T GIVE A SHIT IF ANYONE ELSE SEES THIS.

Something New

Haunting

Your Story

So Many Ideas

Fights

What's Wrong

AND SO..........

Truth

Fool

Focus

Conflict

In Life

HOPE IT ALL WORKS OUT!

Andrews McMeel Publishing
a division of Andrews McMeel Universal
1130 Walnut Street, Kansas City, Missouri 64106
www.andrewsmcmeel.com

24 25 26 27 28 VEP 10 9 8 7 6 5 4 3 2

ISBN: 978-1-5248-9389-7

Library of Congress Control Number: 2024933267

Editor: Lucas Wetzel
Art Director: Diane Marsh
Production Editor: Brianna Westervelt
Production Manager: Chadd Keim

ATTENTION: SCHOOLS AND BUSINESSESS
Andrews McMeel books are available at quantity discounts with bulk purchase for educational, business, or sales promotional use. For information, please e-mail the Andrews McMeel Publishing Special Sales Department: sales@andrewsmcmeel.com.